Great Salt Lake
Regional Book of Facts and Exploration

Alan Millard

Dedicated to those who protect the environment, maintain historical values, and help to preserve the land in its natural state.

Photos were taken by the author, unless otherwise specified.

CONTENTS

INTRODUCTION
- INSIGHT TO A UNIQUE REGION

You are about to be taken from the Pleistocene Ice Age period to the present in a geographic, location offering unique geology, a story preserved in physical geography, and a history that includes first evidence of human presence and tales of great human strife. You will also be exposed to phenomena that demonstrate application of important ecological principles.

This book of facts and discovery takes you from ancient times to present, and ventures from lake to land exploration, and studies life forms as small as bacteria and as big as North America's largest mammals. In your venture, you will discover that the ecological principals applying to this region also apply to other locations and areas of related study. Lake Bonneville, associated physical geography, early history, unique life forms and weather patterns are all included as part of the complete picture. However, a tremendous contrast exists between the present and past in landscape, creatures and culture.

Natural features of the Great Salt Lake region include perspectives not realized, nor understood, by most people. Hidden phenomena are disguised to be something we take for granted: Sandy beaches, sure, but of pearl sand; a large lake, without any fish; shrimp, but of a miniature variety; evidence of a freshwater lake, but in areas of a dry desert; flies, that are only associated with salt water?

Imagine a land before time--a measurement we only know in human terms--covered with large lakes formed from melting Ice Age glaciers. Picture a humid climate with lush vegetation resulting from many years of evaporation and condensation supplying water to lands between these lakes. Lakes, known to us now as Lahontan, Missoula and Bonneville, to mention only a few, reached across vast areas, with smaller, yet significant, bodies of water between them. A strange, contrasting landscape appears compared to what now exists. And the creatures, co-dependent upon the land, are just as foreign to us now as the land in which they lived.

Chapter One

PHYSICAL GEOGRAPHY

Great Salt Lake is the largest of three remnants of ancient Lake Bonneville. Utah Lake, west of Provo, and Sevier Lake, west of Fillmore, make up the other two. Lake Bonneville, a large, freshwater lake, existing 14,500 years ago, was 140 miles wide and 285 miles long, with a depth of at least 1,000'. Its area of coverage consisted of 20,000 square miles, which encompassed almost half of present-day Utah and what are now parts of eastern Nevada and southern Idaho.

This huge lake formed from ice-age glaciers melting and draining into a large basin, in conjunction with volcanic activity occurring mostly around its southern half. What are referred to as benchmarks or terraces are seen throughout the region etched into the landscape and seen on the sides of mountains. Similar to the rings left on the sides of a bathtub, they offer physical evidence of shorelines from the ancient lake levels. Differing from today's environment, a humid climate existed during this time period.

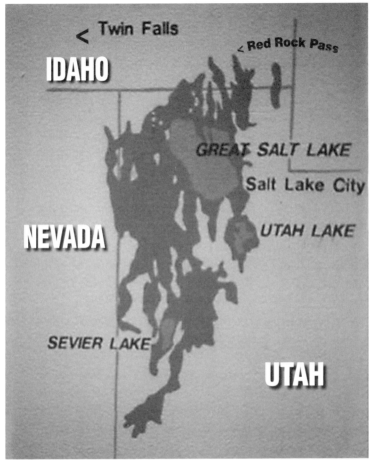

Lake Bonneville compared to present-day remnants and state lines.

Volcanic Activity

As volcanoes helped to form the southern perimeter of the lake, geodes, sometimes called thunder eggs, are found in this area. They result from a complicated process not fully understood by geologists. Several types of geodes develop, which involves crystallization and other chemical processes associated with volcanic activity and aquatic sedimentation.

Geodes

Volcanic activity included underwater volcanoes that emerged from beneath the depths of Lake Bonneville.

Volcanic cones appear where eruptions have shot up through the ancient Bonneville level.

Although Lake Bonneville reached the highest elevation, other lake levels existed before and after Bonneville, with their evidence also etched into the local landscape. The most prominent besides Bonneville are the Provo, Stansbury, and Gilbert levels. The Great Salt Lake presently averages an elevation of 4,200 feet.

Prominent benchmarks reveal the Bonneville (top) and Provo lake levels.

Bonneville Flood

Water exiting Lake Bonneville flowed north into the Snake River drainage system. The extra force created by floodwaters wore away the earth to a less stable rock material that gave way at a place now called Red Rock Pass. This burst of a natural dam had enough physical force to carve out Hell's Canyon in present-day Idaho, and immediately lowered the lake to the Provo level.

This remaining body of water also went through a tremendous transition after human presence. After receding to the Provo level, its water continued to exit through Red Rock Pass. But gradually the excess water source from melting glaciers was depleted, until eventually the evaporation rate was enough to prevent any water from flowing out of the basin. This was the beginning process that formed Great Salt Lake.

As most fresh water contains small quantities of mineral salts, the cumulative factor is immense when we consider the mass quantities of fresh water that are continually deposited into the basin. When water can only escape through evaporation, all of its mineral components are left behind.

Exploration drilling has revealed a thick layer of alluvium sediment deposited on the bottom of Lake Bonneville. A layer of salt at least 20' thick has also been discovered during drilling operations located beneath the floor of Great Salt Lake.

Due to sedimentation later occurring, Lake Bonneville likely had a much greater depth when it was first formed. Sedimentation from the Provo time period also contributed to filling in the basin, and needs to be considered in calculating Lake Bonneville's depth.

Geology

The Farmington Canyon Complex, dating 2.8 - 3 billion-years-old, is a form of Gneiss that represents some of the oldest rock in the world. Antelope Island offers access to these rocks. Located to the south, and beginning at about mid-point on the island, they can be viewed along the eastside road, slightly north of the Frary Peak turn-off.

Forms of conglomerates are medium-aged in comparison, which are included in the Perry Canyon Formation deposited over 700 million years ago.

Tintic Quartzite is relatively new, geologically, and ranges from 570 to 540 million years in age.

Tintic Quartzite

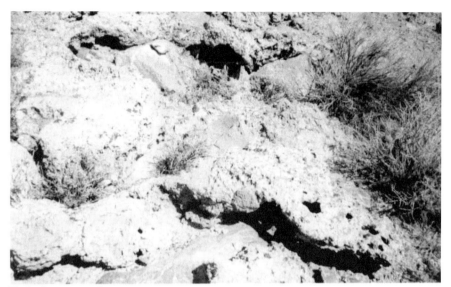

Tufa is some of the most recent rock to be formed, with large quantities evident from the Lake Bonneville level/period.

Oolitic Sand (Pearl Sand) is the newest rock, since it continually forms within the Great Salt Lake. Forming in the shallow offshore water, each grain, called an oolite (egglike), begins from an organic nucleus, usually a brine shrimp fecal pellet, with rings of calcium deposits collecting around it. A constant shift of the sand grains within the lake serves to form and polish them into small, smooth, perfectly rounded balls. Oolitic sand is excellent for sand sculpturing, and has brought many people from the local area and out of state to participate in sand sculpturing contests.

Oolites (sand particles) magnified

"Buda," from Beach Fest '95, is made from oolitic sand. This facility on the south shore is no longer maintained, and is no longer managed by Utah State Parks. Antelope Island is in background.

Chapter Two

The Living Environment: Bonneville Period and Beyond

Fossil remains from the Lake Bonneville era include bones and skeletons of the Musk Ox, Monroc bear, Bonneville cutthroat trout, ancient camel, buffalo, horse, Bighorn Sheep, and Woolly Mammoth. To get a perspective on the size of some of these giants, the Woolly Mammoth towered over the modern-day elephant, and the Monroc Bear was about eight times larger than the common black bear. The Bonneville cutthroat trout lived in the lake until the fresh water changed to saline.

Musk Ox

Ancient Trees and other Vegetation

Huge ferns and gigantic trees existed, similar to Redwoods, which are living remnants ("tree dinosaurs") from the ancient past. In very rare cases, environmental conditions and accommodating geographic locations allowed these trees to survive the last Ice Age. True dinosaurs of the plant world, these trees lived thousands of years ago, with an individual lifespan often exceeding 3,500 years.

Native Cultures

Human presence in the region dates back 12,000 years, which information is due to archaeological evidence discovered at Danger Cave. This cave is located northeast of Wendover, Utah on what used to be the edges of an ancient lake. Humans living 9,000 to 12,000 years ago were referred to as Paleo-Indian/Big Game Hunters. Ancestors to the Fremont, then Shoshone, Ute, Paiute and Goshute Indians, these nomadic groups hunted Pleistocene mammals such as Woolly Mammoths, Bighorn Sheep and ancient camels. What archaeologists refer to as "fluted" projectile points are found in the region. These advanced projectile points were used to take down large mammals. Most, if not all, established caves in the Great Salt Lake region reveal some evidence of early human existence. Hunting the large mammals occurred from about 8,500 to 13,000 years ago, between the Provo and Gilbert lake levels.

Buffalo were present in the Great Salt Lake area until about 1833. Indians adjacent to Great Salt Lake were fortunate to not be heavily dependent on the buffalo as a food supply, with alternative food sources available such as fish, waterfowl, deer, rabbits, antelope, big horn sheep, insect larva and a great diversity of vegetation for consumption. Pine nuts provided an annual staple. The cattail plant was used for food (the tender roots and shoots), as well as for boats, duck decoys and clothing.

Duck decoys discovered in a local cave were dated to be at least 3,000 years old.

A small basket from Danger Cave.

Juke Box Cave is another cave of significant value. Located within a half-mile north of Danger Cave, the cave received its name due to recreational accommodations made for military personnel stationed at Wendover Field during WWII. A juke box was installed in the cave that provided music for dancing on a dance floor that was built in the cave.

Dance floor, with piles of sifted soil left by looters.

Ironically, the concrete dance floor was built over layers of archeological material, which served to protect artifacts and historical stratification. But since looters have been a problem in both caves, and recently discovered these values beneath the floor in Juke Box Cave, both Danger Cave and Juke Box Cave have been barred to prevent further looting.

Petroglyphs inside Juke Box Cave.

Discovery and Exploration

Maps dated as early as 1710, such as the La Hontan Map, named in honor of the explorer Baron La Hontan, acknowledge Great Salt Lake. La Hontan charted his map based on stories from Native Americans about a large, salty lake. Spanish priests, Silvestre V'elez de Escalante and Atanasio Dominguez, in 1776 entered Utah valley through Spanish Fork Canyon. Similar to the previous account, Ute Indians also told them of a very large, salty lake about 50 miles north. Although they too did not see the lake, this specific report on the lake's proximity and condition gave more credit and official documentation accepted by the outside world. Prior to this, the lake was represented on North America maps as a somewhat legendary body of water.

Mountain man, Jim Bridger is credited as the discoverer of Great Salt Lake. By resolving a dispute between other mountain men of where the Bear River flows, he became the first Anglo to reach the lake. With the water found to be saline, the Great Salt Lake was first thought to be an arm of the Pacific Ocean.

The first official survey and exploration of the lake was conducted in 1843 by John Charles Fremont. As a second lieutenant in the Topographical Corps., he was sent to survey the west and map the best route to California. During this expedition, Fremont and his crew, including Kit Carson, who was at the time also a member of the Fremont expedition, came close to drowning in a rubber raft due to a sudden storm that hit while they were on the lake. Kit Carson carved a cross into a rock on Fremont Island, which is well preserved and still visible today.

Photo courtesy of the Stoddard Family.

Fremont also returned to the Great Salt Lake on a later trip to continue area exploration. Howard Stansbury conducted another survey in 1850. During this survey process, red cloth--something that the Indians valued very highly--was used to cover the triangulation station. They swam out to Carrington Island and took the cloth.

Spanish Influence

The Old Spanish Trail
(Santa Fe to Los Angeles, 1829 to 1850.)

Although the Spanish Trail enters the southern boundaries of the Great Salt Lake region, its influence was wide-spread. Along with Spanish presence established prior with the

Domingeuz-Escalante route, the trail maintained a Spanish influence in an area that at one time was owned by Spain. The northern part of the Spanish Trail cut across the Domingeuz-Escalante route in a diagonal east-west direction, making a somewhat half circle through Utah. From south of Moab to Green River, Castle Dale to Salina, and through Richfield to St. George, Utah contains more of the Spanish Trail than any other state. Most areas in this region first visited and named by the Spanish were later renamed by the Mormons.

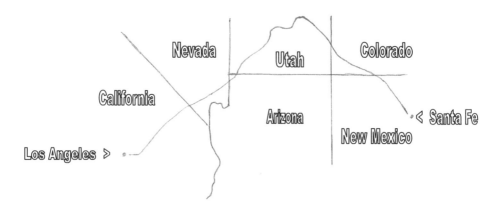

Chapter Three

European Influence

Cultural Conflict and Abuse

Discovery of North and South America by Europeans, with consequent immigration, resulted in a conflict of cultures. Altering nature to fit demands by the new culture conflicted with a lifestyle existing in harmony with the natural environment. Tensions grew, with an intolerance expressed by the intruders. Here, as in many other locations, events took place in an effort to exterminate the native people.

Bear River Massacre

The Bear River Massacre, occurring north of Preston Idaho, is a local example involving the wanton killing of all but 7 of a northwest band of 450 Shoshone Indians by Col. Conner of the California Volunteers on January 29, 1863 (Shoshone-Bannock Tribal Museum, Fort Hall, Idaho).

Similar to how the Jews were treated by the Nazis, this is one of many battles representing a holocaust taking place in North America against its native people. Conner, who was intent on exterminating the Indians, planned to take no prisoners at the Bear River encounter, and intentionally blocked their escape. All but a couple or so trying to escape into the icy river were shot in their attempt. "Outgunned, the Indian men, women, and children fell in heaps before the volunteers" p. 200, Madsen, B.) *The Shoshoni Frontier and the Bear River Massacre.*

Shocking cruelty and torture were also administered to these Shoshone. The wounded and helpless were struck in their heads by axes. Babies and children were killed, and women in the process of dying were raped by the soldiers, with many others experiencing treatment this source considers unspeakable. Some were ravished and brutally killed and sadistically tortured beyond comprehension as many personal accounts testified, with Chief Bear Hunter being tortured to death in the worse fashion one could ever imagine. Conner was commended, and promoted to a brigadier general for this event.

These were Shoshone--Sacajawea's people. Lewis and Clark would have perished, and failed in their mission to the Pacific if it had not been for Sacajawea's help and guidance. Jim Bridger, whose third wife was Shoshone, also lived with the Shoshone and gave great praise to these native people, even in comparison to others. We must also keep in mind that the soldiers' families were not attacked, but the soldiers attacked these Indian families in their homes, killing and torturing all the family members, and then took their belongings. The dead Indians were left in the snow, and their bodies taken by wolves and other scavengers.

Inter-mountain Indian School

Programs were implemented to change Native Americans to become integrated into the white culture. One of these program facilities was the Inter-mountain Indian School at Brigham City that began in 1950 and closed in 1984. It was the Bureau of Indian Affairs' largest boarding school, and part of a chain of programs that began with the DAWES act of 1887.

Not only did they [the Bureau of Indian Affairs] try to move Indian families onto their own plots of land; they also took Indian children away from their families and sent them to boarding schools run by whites, where they believed the young people could be educated to abandon tribal ways. Few Indians were ready for this wrenching change from their traditional collective society to Western individualism. In any case, white administration of the program was so corrupt and inept, and Indian resistance so strong and enduring, that decades later, the government simply abandoned it.

Alan Brinkley, The Unfinished Nation--A Concise History of the American People, p. 455.

Abandoned buildings of the Brigham City Intermountain Indian School site.

The Donner-Reed Immigrant Party

Seeking a short-cut to California, supposedly saving them 300 miles, the Donner-Reed party took the Hastings Cut-off route, named after the author of *The Emigrant's Guide to Oregon and California.* **Reaching the Salt Lake Valley in August 1846, members of this immigrant party had already endured many unnecessary hardships and delays due to poor advice from Lansford Hastings, who was guiding another immigrant party (the Young-Harlan Party) ahead of them. Prior to their descent into the Salt Lake Valley, three members of the Donner-Reed Party, James Reed, Charles Stanton and another man, caught up to Hastings who was camped at Black Rock two days ahead. They persuaded him to come back and show them the right route to take. Having them avoid his own poor choice in routes he and his party had just experienced, he recommended another route, then returned to Black Rock. But what Hastings offered only proved to be more poor advice, causing more delays, taxing labor and unnecessary risks. (Mormon immigrants greatly benefited from their toil the following year, using the route broken by the Donner-Reed Party.)**

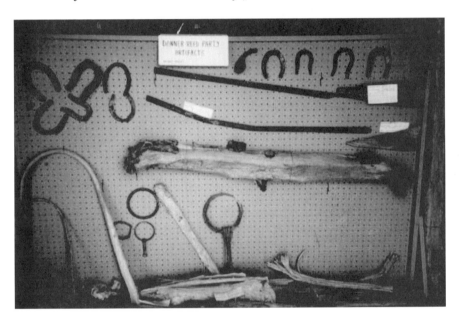

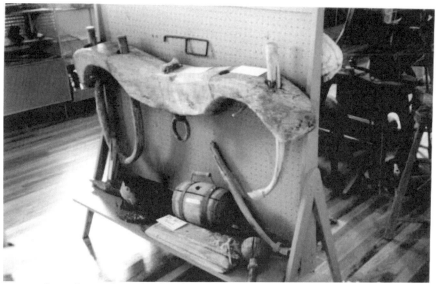

Ox yoke, cask, and other items from the Donner-Reed party.

Many members of the Donner-Reed immigrant party wanted to stay longer in the Salt Lake Valley to recuperate. But time, being of the essence, drove them on. Realizing they must cross the Seirra Nevada Mountains before the winter snows came, and thoughts of having a straight shot and better traveling conditions (a flat stretch), provided them additional motivation to keep moving, stopping basically long enough to graze livestock and replenish supplies. Consisting of a party of 87 immigrants, 66 wagons and a herd of cattle, they headed west across the Great Salt Lake Desert over the Hasting's Cut-off toward Pilot Peak--a guiding landmark used by immigrants in their westward trek. Unfortunately, conditions got worse shortly after they entered the Great Salt Lake Desert. A contrast to their previous environment was soon revealed for which they were not prepared. They had not brought enough water. But this condition was mainly due to more poor advice and inaccurate information received from Hastings concerning the distance across the salt flats, availability of water, and where to locate it. A zigzag effect in their route caused them even further delay.

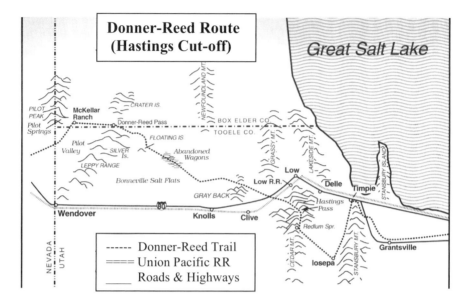

Donner-Reed Route (Hastings Cut-off)

Great Salt Lake

PILOT PEAK
Pilot Springs
McKellar Ranch
CRATER IS.
Donner-Reed Pass
NEWFOUNDLAND MT.
BOX ELDER CO.
TOOELE CO.
FLOATING IS
Pilot Valley
SILVER Is.
Abandoned Wagons
LEPPY RANGE
GRASSY MT.
LAKESIDE MT.
STANSBURY ISLAND
Bonneville Salt Flats
Low
Low R.R.
Delle
Timpie
GRAY BACK
Hastings Pass
Wendover
80
Knolls
Clive
Redlum Spr.
Grantsville
NEVADA UTAH
CEDAR MT.
Iosepa
STANSBURY MT.

------ Donner-Reed Trail
==== Union Pacific RR
____ Roads & Highways

Hastings had left a message at the last watering hole in Skull Valley that had to be pieced together, telling the group that the distance left to travel across the desert was 35-40 miles, when the actual distance was 80 miles. Another unnecessary detour, later imposed by following Hasting's trail, added at least a week to their traveling time. They could see their mountain destination for days, but progress getting to it was hardly noticeable. Pilot Peak is shown from the salt flats.

Worse problems resulted when they entered the final stretch across the salt flats to Pilot Peak. Their wagons, heavy with supplies and valuables, broke through the salt crust and bogged down. And without water, their oxen and other livestock went crazy from thirst and the salt crystals cutting their hooves, and many died. Also, five wagons and many belongings had to be abandoned ten miles after entering the salt flats. One wagon containing the most valuables was well hidden and preserved with apparent intentions of returning for it at a later date.

Before reaching their final California destination, almost half of the Donner Party perished, succumbing to frostbite and starvation, with human upon human predatory acts and cannibalism taking place. A total of 47 members of the party survived.

Black Rock

Black Rock is also the gravesite where John Hargrave, a member of Hasting's group, and Luke Halloran, a member of the Donner-Reed party, were buried. Giving an indication of time delays, Halloran was buried at the same location three weeks after Hargrave's burial. In 1933 the remains of two people, most likely Halloran and Hargrave, were unearthed by highway construction workers at Black Rock. (Black Rock, also the location of a popular resort, and qualifying as an island during high water levels, is pictured in the island and resort sections.)

Mormon Settlement

Arriving in the Salt Lake Valley the following year, Mormon immigrants used the same trail through Immigration Canyon blazed by the Donner-Reed party. Selecting a remote geographic location, free from persecution and one few yet claimed, they settled.

The Mormon leader, Brigham Young, was at first disappointed in the area, feeling misled by Lt. Fremont's journals. However, despite the initial disappointment shared by many, the area revealed good soil, combined with an ample fresh water supply that produced great crops. Bountiful and Farmington are among two towns named for this agricultural value. But due to population expansion and housing development, the most valuable farmland is now being destroyed.

The Mormons were successful at raising food and livestock that they traded and sold to the westbound immigrants. Salt, used for human consumption, was also retrieved from the lake to be used and sold.

Salt Extraction Process and Early Industry

Great Salt Lake provided a good source of salt for the early pioneers, with a salinity level of 25% at the time of their settlement. They could boil four gallons of lake water and receive one gallon of salt. Seizing the opportunity, the Mormon pioneers soon began selling the salt at a premium price to immigrants. Not long after Mormon settlement--in the spring of 1850--a permanent salt-extraction industry became established. Large kettles were first used to boil off the water to retrieve the salt. However, a major salt extraction industry and process began during the 1860s due to the silver mining boom.

A high demand was created for mineral salts contained within Great Salt Lake because they were needed by the mining industry to break down ore deposits. The great quantities of salt needed for this process led to more advanced and efficient methods of salt extraction. Approximately 1.6 million tons are removed from the Great Salt Lake annually.

The Pony Express--Business, Route, Trails and Stations
(April 3, 1860 to October 24, 1861)

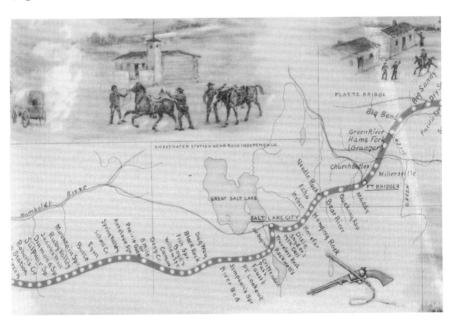

The Pony Express Route consisted of 2-man stations along a dangerous, lengthy trail. These stations were provided at standard, consistent intervals to revive riders and for the feeding, watering, caring and shodding of horses. The station attendants, consisting of the keeper and his assistant, had an isolated and hazardous life. The station keepers were paid $50.00 to $75.00 per month, and the assistants, often referred to as stable boys, were paid close to half that amount. Earth floors, boxes for furniture, roofs not efficient enough to shed the elements, and windows not letting in much light, nor sealed well, describes the living conditions of these stations.

The trail riders had a lonely and dangerous task. First, some were killed out of curiosity by Indians who only found papers in their possession, and who thereafter deemed the riders crazy, which status helped save their lives. Indians considered crazy people sacred, and would therefore not harm them. The Pony Express riders received $120.00 to $125.00 per month in payment for their service.

Golden Spike National Monument

Promontory is the location, and May 10, 1869 is the date, the rails of the transcontinental railroad were joined. Golden Spike National Monument preserves this location, now abandoned by the main railroad route due to the Lucin Cut-off.

Jupiter & Locomotive Number 119 on old railroad grade, May 1996 reenactment.

Chinese Railroad Workers and their Camps

Chinese proved to be more diligent, serious, dependable, self-disciplined and harder workers than the others who were prone to drinking, fighting, and moving on, merely using the railroad as a means to earn some money and relocate near goldfields. The Chinese did as they were told very skillfully and without complaint, even concerning conditions and tasks that few white men would endure. Workers were also hard to attain due to the Civil War.

Beginning with 2,000, the Central Pacific brought in Chinese to work on the railroads. Mr. Crocker, who headed the railroad construction project for the Central Pacific, stated that the Chinese built The Great Wall of China, so they could build the railroad. The Chinese, who were referred to as "Crocker's Pets," camped apart from the other workers, and worked in groups of 20-30. Jealousy existed by the Caucasian workers who hated the Chinese. However, the Chinese did most of the dangerous work, and some were killed during the excavations. (No record of Chinese casualties was kept by the Central Pacific.) After the Chinese proved to be superb workers, recruiters were sent to Asia, resulting in over 12,000 Chinese being hired by the railroad. The white railroad workers were predominantly Irish, and on many occasions it was Irishmen versus Chinamen. And the Chinese workers usually had an Irish boss. Ironically, the Irish accepted the Chinese more willingly once they realized the Chinese did all the "dirty work"-- performed the hardest manual labor and did the most dangerous tasks, allowing the status jobs to be saved for the Irish. Even some of the Irish admired the Chinese for their courage and dedication.

Black powder, being a Chinese invention, was something they knew how to use well, and was used daily in blasting. At the request of the Chinese, who stressed they were accustomed to this type of work, reeds were sent from San Francisco which they wove into baskets. The Chinese, hanging in baskets on the sides of cliffs, bored holes with small hand-drills, placed the powder charges, set and lit the fuse, then hollered to be pulled out of the way. The white laborers couldn't do this. One reporter wrote how mountains resembled ant hills with the Chinese working as a great army, each one staring out from under a large basket hat, like an umbrella. These hats protected the Chinese from the heat as well as other weather conditions. Unlike the white workers, they ate healthy, tasty and well-cooked food. The Chinese bought and prepared all their own food, and didn't drink the water directly from the creeks that made the others sick. They drank only tepid tea from boiled water. The Chinese smoked opium in their spare time, especially Sundays (the only day the workers had off) to relax, but never became intoxicated as was a common occurrence amongst the other workers. They were clean and organized. As for personal hygiene, they took daily sponge baths in warm water, washed their clothes and kept clean and healthy. In contrast, the whites were coined as having a sort of hydrophobia, which caused them to avoid contact with water.

As both east and west bound tracks approached each other, friction mounted. The Union Pacific, not consisting of Chinese, had mostly Irish workers who held contempt for the Central Pacific Chinese. The Irish started fights with the Chinese and occasionally shot them. One might say that the height of adversary show, but in a more civil expression, came when a contest was held between the two railroads to see who could lay the most track in one day. A $10,000 bet was made by Crocker with Durant that the CPRR would win. The contest was won by the Central Pacific, laying 10 miles of track, versus the Union Pacific's 8 miles of track. The eastbound and westbound rails paralleled each other. Congress instructed both railroads to continue construction until their rails met. Dodge proposed meeting at Promontory, but Dorant refused. The railroads were paid $30,00 per mile of track. Congress had to set a place where the rails would meet, which was the location Dorant had originally proposed.

Chinese are excluded from this original photo depicting the meeting of the rails. (Used by permission of the Utah Historical Society.)

The original sign, now preserved under glass. Golden Spike NM.

Every western town had a Chinatown, but most are gone, with their occupants victims of prejudice and discrimination. And it was due to this treatment that the term, "Not a Chinaman's chance" originated. The Chinese would be beat and killed for "fun." The pigtail, very sacred to the Chinese, would be cut off by whites. During this time, Blacks were more protected by law than the Chinese, against whom laws were made, strictly forbidding them from certain employment and many rights held by others. A California tax collector who boasted of killing a Chinaman and of abusing other Chinese, was later appointed by President Grant as ambassador to Japan. Chinese persecution continued in the U.S. to result in the Chinese Exclusion Act passed by U.S. Congress in 1882, and was not repealed until 1952.

Chapter Four

Lake History after European Settlement

Vessels of the Lake
Boating/Freighting and Transcontinental Transport

The Kate Conner, named after the wife of General Conner involved in the Bear River Massacre, was the first steamboat on Great Salt Lake. It transported railroad ties and telegraph poles from the lake's south shore to where they were needed, often traveling the Bear River waterway. Hauling a heavy load of ore, the Kate Conner sank in 1871 on a sandbar in the Bear River.

Two other smaller steamers, the Susie Ritter and Whirlwind, both operated out of Garfield Beach. After a couple of years, the Susie Ritter sank in a storm.

The City of Corrine, a 150 foot steamboat, triple-decked paddle-wheeler, launched on May 22, 1871, was first a workboat that made three runs per week down the Bear River from the Corrine railroad terminal to Tooele Valley. It was bought in 1872 by the Lehigh and Utah Mining Company and converted to an excursion vessel. Later, it was rechristened the General Garfield in honor of a passenger, James Garfield, who later became the 20th president of the United States. Public boating access to Great Salt Lake is limited to two state park facilities—the Antelope Island and Great Salt Lake marinas.

Lake Resorts

   Saltair, one of many original resorts existing around the perimeter of Great Salt Lake, had a hard time surviving, but is now the only remnant of all lake resorts. A modern-day version next to I-80 at exit 104, along with the electric-generator station at the original location 3 miles further east, are all that remain.

Photo used by permission of the Utah Historical Society.

The original Saltair, a major, famous and elaborate resort, opened in 1893, but burned down in 1925. It had a huge dancefloor built upon springs, and hosted famous bands such as Guy Lumbardo. It was rebuilt, and the second version burned down in 1971. In 1981, a new Saltair was built when Wally Wright and three other business partners bought a 30,000 sq. foot aircraft hanger from Hill Air Force Base, which provided the basic structure for the present Saltair version that opened in 1983. However, later that same year it was flooded by the '83-'87 rise in Great Salt Lake. Its parking lot for a short time thereafter served as the lake's marina, harboring mostly sailboats. Saltair again reopened in 1993, and currently continues to operate.

The first lake resort, _Lake Side_, was opened in 1870 near Farmington by one of Brigham Young's sons, John W. Young. The resort was later moved inland in 1894 due to a receding lake level to eventually become present-day Lagoon.

Lake Point Resort, located near the present town of Lake Point, later moved east to become Garfield Beach Resort.

Garfield Beach Resort was home port to the General Garfield paddle-wheeler excursion boat. Being non-Mormon owned and operated, it was considered taboo by church officials. The resort was located west of Black Rock on the south shore of Great Salt Lake.

Black Rock Resort, located at Black Rock, was a popular railroad destination for many tourists. It operated from 1880 to 1959--longer than any other lake resort.

A skim of ice on lake's surface--looking west toward I-80/Blackrock, with Stansbury Mountains in background. This is the major resort strip along the south shore west of Saltair, where little evidence now exists of any lake resort.

Sunset Beach Resort was located between Black Rock and Saltair.

Lake Park Resort, located along the eastern shore near Farmington, operated from 1886 to 1895.

Syracuse Beach Resort, located north of the Antelope Island causeway entrance station, operated from 1887 to 1891. Other small resorts came and went.

Chapter Five

Recent Lake History

Lucin Railroad Cut-off

This short-cut across the Great Salt Lake, from west of Ogden to Lakeside, was originally built in 1903. It saved the railroad time, distance and grades. A 12-mile stretch of trestle was necessary along this route due to very unstable ground--the deepest trough with ancient sentiment underlying the lake's floor.

Original railroad trestle across 12-mile stretch of Great Salt Lake.

Despite the lake water only being 20-30' deep, due to the unstable medium, approximately 38,000 pilings, each 120' long and made of old-growth Douglas Fir, were driven into the lake's floor to secure a sound foundation for the railroad. Although most were driven 120 feet to secure a sound footing, many of these pilings had to be placed end to end (240') to secure the trestle.

Construction of the present-day causeway, consisting of a solid rock fill, with two 15-foot culverts, was started in 1955 and completed in 1959 by the Southern Pacific Railroad. The Little Valley construction camp was located approximately 2 miles north of Promontory Point near the site that was blasted in July 1957 to get the rock needed for fill. The project cost over $50 million.

Ramifications of the Railroad Causeway

As a result of this man-made barrier, the Great Salt Lake became divided into a northern and southern arm. During the start of the flood years in 1984, so much water was entering the southern arm that the causeway was acting as a dam. An additional 300' opening was blasted through the causeway in 1984 to allow more water to flow into the north arm. The lake's dynamics were not fully understood when this construction project was planned, including the consequences underlying that 90% of all fresh water from tributaries first enters the south arm. (Refer to ecological section for further detail concerning this natural phenomenon.)

Effect on Lake's Ecology

The Lucin Cut-off saved the railroad many miles and displaced steep grades with a flat surface.

Dismantling of railroad trestle: Notice the solid rock fill (causeway) north through the trestle pilings, with abandoned railroad cars. These cars were used by the railroad to shore up the causeway during the flood years.

Allowing lake water to freely exchange between the north and south parts of the lake, the railroad trestle was compatible with the Great Salt Lake ecosystem. Not until a solid rock fill replaced the trestle were any negative effects evident on the lake's ecology. Due to 90% of the lake's water (mainly tributaries) entering south of the railroad causeway, the division required the water to flow north in order to reach the part of the lake cut off by the railroad's rock fill. This division has greatly altered the ecology of Great Salt Lake ever since. The northern arm now being a depository of mineral salts, has created a lucrative opportunity for northern Great Salt Lake mineral extraction companies, but has permanently changed the lake's ecology.

The flood years were from 1983 to 1987. In '86 and '87 the lake reached an elevation barely under 4,212'. During this time period the southern arm of Great Salt Lake became so diluted that few brine shrimp eggs hatched. However, with the northern arm of Great Salt Lake being too saline "normally" for brine shrimp eggs to hatch, the dilution caused it to lower to a salinity level that again supported brine shrimp. A salinity level of 16%

is close to ideal, with the northern arm usually about 10% more saline than the southern arm of the lake, often maxing out at 27.3% (saturation point).

West Desert Pumping and Evaporation Project

Due to Great Salt Lake's rising waters during the mid '80s, the West Desert Pumping Project resulted. Areas adjacent to the lake were being flooded, which included wildlife refuges, boat harbors, state and federal highways, and the Salt Lake International Airport.

At first, a law was passed deeming the flood illegal. One proposed plan was to divert water from the Bear River into the Snake River drainage system.

A 320,000-acre area called the Newfoundland Evaporation Basin was developed in 1987 northeast of Wendover into which excess water was pumped from the Great Salt Lake.

West Desert Pumps. (Courtesy of Ron Ollis, Utah Div. of Water Resources.)

Massive, French-made pumps were installed on the west shore of Great Salt Lake within a 4.1 mile canal that parallels the north side of the Southern Pacific Railroad causeway. Although this plan alleviated the problem, within two years the basin was full, with no place left for the water to go. Not enough water evaporated in this process to keep ahead of the flood. The excess water pumped from the north arm of the lake to the west desert was flowing back into the lake. Corresponding to this bleak situation, by mere chance, conditions causing the excess lake water discontinued. This whole project cost $60 million.

Tell-tale remnants of flood clinging to hog-wire fence.

Chapter Six

Bonneville Salt Flats

The Bonneville Salt Flats consist of flat, vast areas of salt. These salt deposits are remnant of past lake levels. Shrinkage in water mass is due to a decreased water supply to a constant evaporation rate ratio. With this effect, combined with fresh water contributing small amounts of mineral salts over thousands of years, mass quantities of salt deposits are left exposed. However, due also to other prior lake levels and sedimentation, thick, hard layers of salt have been discovered deep under the Great Salt Lake. This recent discovery adds more than speculation to the depth of Lake Bonneville possibly being more than 1,000' deep.

The salt desert is quite bleak. Although no plantlife exists in the salt of the actual salt flats, it is present within the less saline desert environment adjacent to them.

View looking east across salt flats from Wendover (Nevada side).

One must keep in mind that water in this arid region also precipitates toward the surface of the soil, bringing mineral salts from beneath the ground to the surface. These are then re-deposited to the lowest point by wind or water transport. The salts are also trapped in some desert areas where a lot of alkali soil exists and fresh water is hard to come by - a factor many pioneers had to face.

Bonneville Speedway

The Bonneville Raceway is located within the Bonneville Salt Flats about 8 miles northeast of Wendover, Utah where the highest land speed record of 622.4 mph was set in 1970 by the Blue Flame. The idea of the salt flats' racing potential originated in 1896 by W.D. Rishel who was scouting a bicycle race course from New York to San Francisco. Rishel later convinced Teddy Tezlaff, a noted daredevil, to attempt an automobile speed record on the salt flats. Tezlaff, driving a Blitzen Bebz in 1914, set an unofficial land speed record of 141.73 mph. David Abbot (Ab) Jenkins from Salt Lake City later promoted the Bonneville Salt Flats as a speedway. Beginning in 1925, he and three Englishmen - Sir Malcolm Cambell, John Cobb and George E.T Eyston - competed on the salt flats to acheive land speed records. In the 1930s, and thereafter, the Bonneville Salt Flats became world famous for racing. On Labor Day 1950, Jenkins broke 26 world records at a top speed of 199.19 mph with his car, the Mormon Meteor III, which is displayed in the Utah State Capitol.

Bonneville Speedway: Speed Week 1995, Wendover, Utah.

Wendover Field Military Facility

During World War II, 20,000 military personnel were stationed at the Wendover Field military facility, located in the southeast outskirts of Wendover, Utah, adjacent to the Bonneville Salt Flats. This is where the atomic bomb was assembled that was dropped on Japan ending WWII. It is also the home hangar of the plane, the Enola Gay, that dropped the bomb.

Enola Gay Hangar

The military bombing range once included areas within the boundaries of Danger Cave State Park and adjacent that had a route (rail line) through which "Tokio Trolley"—a small rail car, with three mounted machine guns—was sent at speeds up to 40mph. Three firing pits in the distance each had a wooden track system through which jeeps, protected from gunfire by pit walls, were sent with mounted targets appearing above them. These provided moving targets for the gunners.

Topaz--The Japanese Internment Camp

Shortly after the Japanese attacked Pearl Harbor, the United States Government declared all Americans of Japanese ancestry to be enemy agents. In both the U.S. and Canada people of Japanese decent were herded into internment camps.

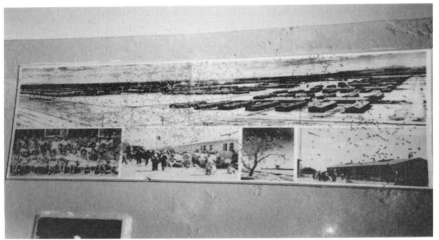

Little evidence now exists of the Japanese encampment once located north of Delta, called The Jewel of the Desert.

First gathered and placed in the horse stables of Tanforan, California, over 8,000 Japanese American men, women and children were shipped by trains to Delta, Utah. After this, they were transported by covered trucks north to a place called Topaz. The camp's title originated due to a nearby mountain bearing the name.

One of the first, most noteworthy conditions was the amount of alkali dust in the living quarters and in the air. These Japanese people, often looking as though they had fallen into a flower barrel, as one woman stated, were subjected to continuous alkali dust. Two inches of the white, powdery dust had to be removed from within the living quarters.

The Japanese were told they were being protected from

non-Japanese people, but conditions and matching sentiment did not match this claim. Guns were pointed at them instead of outward, as one man put it. The guards commonly expressed disrespect and abuse. Shots had been fired upon the people and at least one person was shot for trying to escape. [Later investigation revealed that the individual had been granted a work release to leave the camp for a job in the east, and was shot while placing his hands above his head as he was leaving.]

Shortly after this incident, the American Japanese were given a choice to go back into society under the condition they swear allegiance to the United States. All the young men of age, who swore their allegiance, had to enlist in the military and contribute to the war effort. Due to their assignments, these young men received some of the highest casualty rates of the war. After the end of their 1,146 days of incarceration, the Japanese Americans who returned home found their homes, property, and possessions gone, looted or destroyed.

Of the approximately eight thousand American Japanese, fourteen hundred who felt violated by their own government, refused to give their allegiance to the U.S.* These people were sent to other internment facilities.

Could this not happen again against another segment of our population that is deemed by popular prejudice to be less worthy or valuable? Those who can not remember the past are condemned to repeat it. George Santayana, *Reason and Common Sense*

[*Foot Note: One may also wonder if some of the Japanese lacked allegiance to the U.S. before their internment. And, if so, how do these numbers compare to those who lacked allegiance after their internment? Although not unwarranted, was this refusal to give allegiance to the U.S. entirely a result of the treatment they received, or were some supporters of Japan included within this category from the start?]

Chapter Seven

Islands of Great Salt Lake

About a dozen islands exist on the Great Salt Lake at any given time. By receding water levels, some islands are formed by land being exposed while at the same time other land areas, previously surrounded by water, connect to the mainland. Or, a higher water elevation covers up some islands and surrounds others. Starting with the largest, islands of the Great Salt Lake include: Antelope, Stansbury, Fremont, Carrington, Gunnison, Dolphin, Hat or Bird Island, Badger, Cub, White Rock, Egg, and conditionally, Black Rock, Strong's Knob and Goose.

Island inhabitants included the Fremont and later, their descendents, the Utes and Shoshones. Recent digs on Antelope Island have revealed many centuries of seasonal visits due likely to fall hunting parties. But as far as researchers can determine, no permanent occupancy existed on any of the islands. However, ample evidence reveals that many inhabitants lived year-round adjacent to Great Salt Lake. The shores of Farmington Bay are rich in evidence of ancient human occupancy.

Antelope Island

   Antelope Island, **16 miles long and an average of 3.5 miles wide, is the largest island within Great Salt lake, and the largest state park in Utah, consisting of 28,000 acres, with its highest elevation at 6,597 feet. The island received its name due to a successful antelope hunt by Fremont's surveying party. A marina exists at the island's northern end on the north side of the causeway.**

Antelope Island causeway, marina and memorial. Notice curvature of the causeway. With a curve being stronger than a straight line, the causeway was designed to shed forces and withstand storms from every direction.

Antelope Island visitor center

In the Spring of 1999, while preparing to install the current water system at Mushroom Springs for the Garr Ranch, an archeological site was discovered. One of the most valuable assets to this discovery was the distinct stratification--layers marking the times the camp was occupied--that revealed recurring visits for hundreds of years. According to archeological research, with digs beginning in 1999, the island's first occupants were hunters, with occupancy occurring seasonally on a yearly basis. The site revealed charcoal (evidence of fires), shards, arrow points, deer bones, bowls, manos and metates.

Though native inhabitants did not understand the idea of owning land, Chief Wanship's son and his three wives had claim to the island as their hunting grounds. A deal was made by Fremont, granting Wanship's son with trade goods after he found out about Fremont's successful hunt.

Fielding Garr began building the Garr Ranch in 1848. He was commissioned as a licensed herdsman by Brigham Young to raise cattle to support the Perpetual Immigration Fund, which generated funds to finance Mormon immigration to Utah. The money would be paid back to the fund after the immigrants were established. However, most of the island's ownership was not by the Mormon church. The ranch later changed hands, with the John Dooly family owning it until 1972, when it was acquired by the Anschutz family. Then, in 1981 for the price of $4,700,000, the whole island was acquired as a state park.

Notice succession of adobe brick from left, 1848 to 1880, and the white-painted cinder block, 1950, on the right/north end.

A school by day, bunkhouse by night, and a church on Sunday, with a root cellar in the bottom.

Spring house, and inside Spring house (early-day refrigerator).

Fawns sheltered by their mother in the ranch house barn.

Buffalo on Antelope Island, with Farmington Bay and Wasatch Mountains in background.

Wagon rides at the ranch house.

Army/Air Force Memorial

Located at the west end, and on the north side, of the Antelope Island causeway is the Army/Air Force Memorial. On October 29, 1992, at 9:11pm, one of four military helicopters (a USAF HH-60G) on a training mission, loaded with 13 servicemen, crashed into the Great Salt Lake. The incident took place 300 yards north of the causeway on the north tip of Antelope Island. Only the pilot survived.

Stansbury Island, named in honor of Captain Howard Stansbury, is the second largest island, consisting of 22,314 acres, and reaches the highest in elevation at 6,645 feet. Part of the island is privately owned, and the remainder is managed by the Bureau of Land Management. The BLM and Utah State Parks jointly administer a biking trail that encircles the island by following the Lake Bonneville terrace.

Fremont Island, named for John Fremont, is the third largest island, consisting of 2,945 acres and an elevation of 4,995'. Ponies ran wild on the island for many years until recently. The cross Kit Carson carved while with the Fremont expedition, pictured in chapter two, is located on the island. John Baptise, a convicted Salt Lake City grave-robber, was exiled to Fremont Island in 1862. From 1886 to 1891 a Judge Wenner and his family lived on the island. His grave is there, with his wife's ashes buried beside it. In addition, two natives, an 18-year-old and a 6-year-old, are other burials discovered on the island. Earl Stoddard was the first to begin what has become one of the most unique archeological collections, originating from Fremont Island. Referred to as the Stoddard Collection, it was secured for display in 1999 by the author from the Stoddard family, and is currently an exhibit at the Antelope Island Visitor Center.

Fremont archeological (Stoddard) collection.

Fremont Island silhouetted against Promontory Mountains in background. Egg Island, foreground.

Carrington Island, consisting of 1,767 acres, was named in honor of Albert Carrington who was assigned from the local Mormon community to assist Howard Stansbury's survey. In 1932, Charles Stoddard, trying to raise sheep, built a cabin on the island, and lived there with his wife and three small children.

Due to a lack of freshwater and predation by coyotes, he was not successful. The island has been used more recently as a bombing range by the U.S. Air Force. During low water levels, it is connected with Badger Island.

Gunnison Island consists of 163 acres, with an elevation of 4,492'. Planting 1,000 grape vines, Alfred Lambourne homesteaded the island in the 1890s for the purpose of creating a vineyard. He abandoned the project when he discovered not enough water existed to support their growth. The island is now a rookery for the American White Pelican. Due to state regulation, the island is closed to public access from within a mile of the shoreline.

Dolphin Island, named for being shaped like a dolphin, consists of 60 acres and has an elevation of 4,275'.

Hat or Bird Island, being 22 acres, with an elevation of 4,275', is shaped like a hat and serves as a nesting area for gulls and pelicans. Due to state regulation, this island is also closed to public access from within a mile of its shoreline.

Badger Island, consisting of 6 acres at an elevation of 4,225', is located off the northwest point of Stansbury Island. These two islands are connected by a dike and roadway.

Cub Island, located just north of Gunnison Island in the north arm of the lake, is also a rookery and closed to public access.

White Rock, basically a large rock in the midst of White Rock Bay, serves as a nesting site for California Gulls. Its name is derived from being covered white with sea gull feces.

Egg Island, hardly an acre, depending on the lake's level, is named for the 76 heron eggs taken by Howard Stansbury's men during the lake's early exploration. Closed to public access from April through June, the island is a rookery for the California Gull and Great Blue Heron.

Black Rock not only qualifies as an island during high lake levels, but is a significant historical landmark, first serving as a camping spot and gravesite for immigrants, then a stop along the Overland Stage Route, and later, a popular railroad stop for tourists when the resort was in operation.

Strong's Knob, located in the northwestern part of the lake, also qualifies as an island during high lake levels.

Goose Island, located in the southern part of the lake, is hardly more than a sand bar, or unnoticed when covered by higher water levels. But significance bears witness to it being named an island.

Chapter Eight

Lake Excursions, Other Marinas and Recreational Opportunities

Great Salt Lake Marina

Sail boats docked at the Great Salt Lake Marina.

The Great Salt Lake State Marina (formerly Great Salt Lake State Park) is located east of Black Rock and west of Saltair along Interstate 80. The marina can accommodate about 250 boats, and is the port for lake excursions.

Salt Island Adventures is a tour service of the Great Salt Lake that operates out of the Great Salt Lake Marina. Pictured here is the Island Serenade.

Antelope Island Marina

The marina at Antelope Island is smaller than the Great Salt Lake Marina. It provides accommodations for boaters from the north. Brine shrimpers operate out of both marinas during the winter months, harvesting brine shrimp eggs.

Willard Bay

Willard Bay State Park borders I-15 on the eastern edge of Willard Bay--a diked, fresh water bay adjacent to Great Salt Lake. No boating access exists to Great Salt Lake from Willard Bay. Built just above the Great Salt Lake flood plain, its 9,900 acres of fresh water provide recreational opportunities that include boating, water-skiing and fishing for walleye, crappie, catfish and wiper. Day-use and camping facilities are also available at the park. Besides a north marina, the park also has a south marina that is open from April through October.

Other Areas of Conservation Interest

Many bird refuges and water fowl management areas exist adjacent to the lake in the marshy/wetland areas, including the Layton Wetlands Preserve, Farmington Bay Waterfowl Management Area and the Bear River Migratory Bird Refuge. The Ogden Nature Center is a wildlife preserve in West Ogden off of 12th Street. It is built with wood salvaged from the railroad trestle.

Photo used by permission of the Ogden Nature Center

Chapter Nine

High Desert Environment of the Great Salt Lake Region

Wildlife

Wildlife found in this environment include bobcat, coyotes, badger, sage grouse, jack rabbits (common hare) and Desert Cottontail rabbits. Quail are also present along active irrigation canals where food and adequate cover is available. Ring-neck Pheasants are present in cultivated farmland areas, and Chukar partridge exist in remote rocky areas. Mule deer are evident throughout the region at a variety of elevations. Desert Bighorn Sheep prefer the high rocky elevations.

A Desert Cottontail hanging out.

A mother Pronghorn with her young.

Pronghorn Antelope prefer the wide-open stretches, and are often seen in the valleys away from human habitation. I-80 travelers can often spot Pronghorn Antelope between Grantsville and the salt flats.

Elk are found in the higher elevations. Those closest to the lake are in the Kennecott herd. Moose are also present in some of the more isolated and extensive mountain aquatic environments.

In marshy, wetland areas adjacent to the lake, live raccoon, muskrat, fox, skunks and weasel. Beaver are usually found along creeks and rivers in the higher elevations where fresh water and tress are available.

Buffalo were in the Salt Lake area until about 1833, and vanished from the region during the 1840s, with the last herd existing north of the Bear River country. Chief Wanship recalled seeing buffalo cross to Antelope Island during low lake levels, grazing there, and then returning to the mainland.

Buffalo herd roaming on southeast area of Antelope Island.

One of the highest and most diverse concentrations of wildlife in the lake area exists on Antelope Island. As a wildlife park, it winters approximately 700 hundred buffalo. The herd increases annually from births to about 850 animals by late fall, from which about 150 of the older stock are thinned annually. Of these, five or six of the older bulls are hunted and shot, and the rest of the animals are sold. By this type of management, the herd is kept young and fit.

Between 60 to 75 Pronghorn Antelope live on the island. Giving the island back its namesake, in 1995 state park and wildlife officials transported 42 Pronghorn Antelope onto Antelope Island. Twelve more were added in 1998.

Predation on the baby antelope by coyotes has been very high. Wanting to keep the natural balance, but also wanting the antelope herd to maintain and increase in size, research and studies have been done to address the problem. Other locations experiencing similar predatory problems with coyotes have revealed that certain individuals ("problem dogs"), developing a taste/habit, will predate more heavily than others on antelope fawns. [A note to consider is the antelope fawn is not available as a consistent food source. By only being available during a brief window of time, a natural dependency doesn't exist.]

Introduced to Antelope Island in 1997, California Bighorn Sheep have increased from 23 to about 100.

Elk were introduced to Antelope Island in 1993, but due mainly to improper introduction procedures, they panicked during the transition process, with many heading directly into the lake. Some of the animals died in the lake, and others made it to islands then died. One stayed on the island and hung out with the buffalo until recently. Several made it to the southern end of Great Salt Lake and joined the Kennecott elk herd.

During this time period, while assistant park manager of Great Salt Lake State Park, the author witnessed several elk in the salty waters of the lake just east of the marina—an environment very foreign to elk.

A desert dust devil.

Blending into the surroundings, this oasis can only be detected from a few yards away.

Grassy Mountain rest area, I-80.

Badger raiding bird feeder.

Vegetation

Sage brush, often combined with rabbit brush, is prevalent vegetation throughout the high desert environment. Utah Juniper is often mixed with the sage brush in the slightly higher elevations. Desert flowers are prevalent in the spring, and are plentiful on Stansbury and Antelope Islands.

Indian Paint Brush

Sego Lily (Utah State Flower)

Evening Primrose

Utah Juniper

Although the Utah Juniper is a very common tree found in Utah--its namesake--the official state tree of Utah is the Colorado Blue Spruce.

Pinion Pine

Pinion Pines are small pine trees that are well known in the Southwest for their edible seeds (pine nuts) produced every fall. These trees are often associated with, and dispersed amongst, Utah Juniper in what are called Pinion/Juniper forests throughout Utah and much of the Southwest. The precipitation requirements for the Utah Juniper are less than for the Pinion Pine, so the last tree species seen before relenting to the complete sagebrush environment will usually be the Utah Juniper, often seen growing within the sagebrush community. As a Bureau of Land Management forester pointed out, I-80 is the general northern boundary for the Pinion Pine. (An exception exists in southern Idaho in the vicinity of the City of Rocks (a section of the California Trail) where a Pinion Pine forest exists.)

Cultural Value and Food Source

Also a part of this desert environment are the human native inhabitants, who include a cultural history involving the Pinion Pine and Utah Juniper environment. The Pinion Pine has provided a significant food source (pine nuts) to natives for many centuries. Both the Pinion Pine and Utah Juniper have provided sources for medicinal purposes, as well as shelter and firewood. However, often regarded as a "mother tree," providing a food source as well as a medicinal purpose, the Pinion Pine was usually spared. Only in desperation was the tree cut down and used for firewood by the Indians.

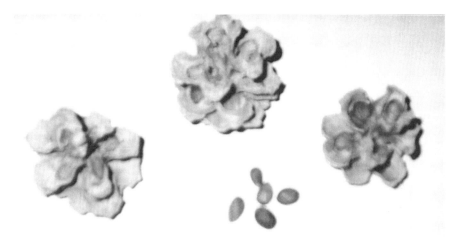

Great Salt Lake Watershed

Another unique feature of the Great Salt Lake region is that beginning at its lowest elevation–the lake and surrounding area, including the salt flats–the environment is very bleak, with no vegetation, but revealing a striking contrast in transition, progresses in elevation to some well-vegetated areas with fair-sized timber. An increase in land elevation above the desert floor corresponds to an increase in the amount and types of vegetation, which is due to more precipitation and cooler summer temperatures.

The Stansbury Mountains south of Stansbury Island reveal this contrast closest to the lake. To the east, in the Wasatch range of the Rocky Mountains, the forested environment is also prevalent. Elevations further west of Wendover include Utah Juniper, large stands of Pinion Pine, and isolated areas of White Fir and Quacking Aspen.

Aspen mixed with Douglas Fir--Stansbury Mountains.

In limited contrast to the desert environment are areas in the mountains where, in many cases, trees are seen only growing on the north slope, or in other shaded areas. In this sun-sheltered environment, with a variation depending on elevation, one will find White Fir, Lodge Pole Pine, Colorado Blue Spruce, Englemann Spruce, Limber Pine, Douglas Fir, Gambel (Scrub) Oak, Ponderosa Pine, maple and aspen. Areas, although high in elevation, are bare of trees due to lacking consistent and adequate moisture.

By the shadows of other mountains and protection from over-exposure to the sun on a northerly slope, snow deposits provide continual moisture to harbor an environment supporting trees and pockets of forests.

Recognizing and Understanding an Altered Environment

Effects of poor Land Management by Over-grazing

Typical of other areas in the region, Antelope Island offers an example of over-grazing by domestic livestock. In the early part of the century, there were over 10,000 sheep on Antelope Island. Cheat grass--a non-native grass species that provides evidence of over-grazing--is prevalent.

Due to overgrazing in a fragile desert environment, cheat grass takes hold as the dominant vegetation, with native species relenting to its endurance and adaptability. Perennial grasses have been reintroduced on Antelope Island in an attempt to replace the cheat grass that now occupies vast areas previously supporting the perennial species. Cheat grass will sometimes crowd out sagebrush by not allowing the seedlings to become established. It is an annual grass species that is only palatable for a two to three week period in the early spring, and thereafter goes to seed and dries up early in the season, using to its full advantage the best part of the growing season. With a kindled setting made by the cheat grass, many fires readily result from lightning strikes. Although an undesirable species concerning its value to wildlife, livestock and general environmental health compared to perennial grasses that help hold more moisture in the soil, cheat grass is more adapted to a harsh environment. It grows fast and uses moisture more efficiently than perennial grasses. The short lifespan of this annual grass species allows it to expend, without risk, all its energy in a brief time period, since it has no need to build reserves to endure the winter as does a perennial species. Quickly going to seed, its life ends by mid-summer. Often, with the right conditions, however, these seeds will germinate in the fall, with seedling growth making use of the available fall moisture to get a head-start for the following spring.

However, ironically, if it weren't for this undesirable species, the top soil would completely erode, and leave the land without the ability to support any vegetation. The cheat grass at least helps to stabilize the soil when no other plant species exist. An extreme desert environment is usually caused by over-grazing. A desert consisting of nothing more than sand or extremely depleted vegetation within an arid environment is seldom a natural occurrence. For example, the Sahara Desert is man-made, caused mostly by sheep overgrazing the landscape.

Knolls. Scars from off-highway-vehicles (OHVs) mark the hillside landscape. Notice sand dunes on left side of photo.

What's called the "Little Sahara," west of Nephi, managed by the Bureau of Land Management, is a popular sand dune/OHV area.

Because of harsh, dry conditions, an arid environment is very sensitive to any alterations, and slower to recover than the continual moist organic soil in a more humid region. After an area dries out completely and loses the ability to maintain any ground cover, a self-destructive process begins that spreads like a cancer, which is especially enhanced by further human activity. Wind takes sand from exposed areas and literally sandblasts adjacent areas. Seeds fail to properly germinate due to a lack of continual moisture or soil to hold them. After the vegetation is removed, the roots dry up and get hard, losing their ability to stabilize the soil. The soil bakes and hardens, or is blown away to leave hardened clay or bare rock. Sand dunes are not uncommon. Rain comes usually fast and hard in this environment, which serves to break up and wash away the weakened soil and remaining plant life. The bleached, sun-baked earth, with no buffer-type surface (topsoil and plant life--similar to a damp sponge) can not readily absorb the water, so water under these conditions often only serves to cause more damage. This is especially true when the rain is mixed with hail, which is a common occurrence.

Healed erosion--scars likely resulting from a time of overgrazing by 10,000 sheep. Antelope Island.

Original Environment witnessed by the First Pioneers

Another part of history seldom told concerns the original condition of the environment. The sage brush country we witness today is very different from the original landscape. A more lush, vegetated environment existed. Early immigrants described seeing vast areas of high, thick grasses, and an actual prairie environment. Between Ruby Valley, in present-day Nevada, and Camp Floyd, in present-day Utah, grasses were reported to be

6-7 feet high, and in some areas, 10-12 feet high. (p. 13. *The Shoshoni Frontier and the Bear River Massacre*)

Cattle soon depleted the grass, which was over-grazed to the point of no return, with total devastation and elimination corresponding to the buffalo that fed upon it, and to the natives who were dependent upon the buffalo. But when time passes and few references exist—photos, personal accounts by people who passed through—little knowledge exists to demonstrate the comparison, and less is therefore passed on to new generations.

One old-timer explained that his father when a boy came out west and witnessed the Utah countryside being very lush with vegetation. He said that sagebrush was present, but seldom seen. He described a prairie environment, with tall grasses, without the gullies and dry washes. He also stressed that wagons could not have passed over the routes they originally traveled if the present-day conditions had existed. Cattle and sheep originated with the pioneers, along with a fierce desire to cut down trees and forests. Many immigrants who came after these first arrivals, although still considered early pioneers, never saw the true, original condition of the natural environment. Before long, little vegetation (ground cover) was left, which exposed the ground, initiating the erosion process that created the lack of native vegetation and the baron, gullied landscape common today. The land could no longer sustain itself in its natural state.

This same abuse applied to the forested country, with the pioneers using trees for desperately needed firewood and lumber. The railroads alone harvested entire forests in a matter of days for railroad ties and fuel to run the locomotives. Miners were also among the first to arrive in mountainous/forested regions. Mining activity caused allot of trees to be used. Hillsides and large tracks of land were completely deforested near mining areas. The mines required timber supports, lumber for dwellings and ore cars, and ties for the ore tracks. And a mass quantity of firewood was necessary for cooking and heating in mining camps and towns.

Early immigrants living on Antelope Island claimed in

their self-sufficiency that all the fence posts used on the island were from trees that grew on Antelope Island. There were over a thousand fence posts.

Another important point to consider is the deterioration of the water resources by domesticated livestock. Differing from wildlife, domestic livestock defecate in their own water supply (drinking water). Many areas, including riparian zones, visited by sheep and cattle are unsuitable for wildlife, and the water resources become contaminated. This factor, combined with the effects of erosion from over-grazing and a damaged watershed from mining operations, further contributes to a negative impact on the environment.

Sure, the country was arid. But has it become drier? Increased vegetation perpetuates more humidity (holds in moisture), and in turn helps to sustain a more vegetated environment for a longer period, with conditions to include perennial grasses that are deeper rooted and higher growing, producing thicker vegetation that can endure normal periods of drought. Could not the modern-day conditions created by poor land-use practices cause longer droughts, accompanied by higher temperatures with less humidity? Once the deterioration process begins, the negatives self-perpetuate.

Chapter Ten

LAKE ENVIRONMENT

Ecology

Basically, the only life that exists within Great Salt Lake are brine shrimp, brine flies, algae, bacteria, protozoa, and a type of water beetle, the corixid.

Great Salt Lake, with Antelope Island in the background.

Although few life forms live in Great Salt Lake, they are very numerous, with the two prominent varieties, the brine shrimp and the brine fly, opposite in character. The brine shrimp is a crustacean and the brine fly is an insect.

Brine Shrimp

Brine Shrimp are miniature shrimp, about 1/3 to ½ of an inch long, that hatch in the spring from eggs that lie dormant over winter. They significantly contribute as a food source to millions of birds that visit Great Salt Lake as part of their annual migrations.

Brine shrimp eggs are so small that about 150 can fit on the head of a pin. The eggs are carried in a pouch at the rear of the female's body. After the eggs hatch, the nuplii form into adults in 2-3 weeks. They also reproduce every 2-3 weeks, at which time they lay approximately 150 eggs. When winter comes, they die off, but leave their eggs to perpetuate their existence. The small, round eggs can remain dormant and fertile for many years, and will not hatch unless conditions are favorable, which includes warm water temperatures in the spring and an adequate salinity level.

Commercial Harvest and Industry

During the winter months, when the brine shrimp eggs are dormant, they are commercially harvested, processed, dried, packaged and sold for fish food. Most are shipped to the orient where they are hatched to feed prawns, crabs and lobsters. Some are bought to provide food for prawn farms in Las Vegas that produce prawns to feed casino visitors. Others are hatched and raised into adults that are processed into fish food (flakes) for home aquariums. About 12.5 million pounds of eggs are harvested annually, which produces an average income of $30 million. The eggs float on the water's surface. Brine shrimp eggs were first gathered by raking them up from the shores of the lake after being consolidated by the wind pushing them into "slicks" and against the lake's shore. They are now gathered by booms, as the brine shrimpers use the same process developed to collect and dispose of oil slicks in the harvesting process.

Brine shrimp eggs floating on water's surface.

Brine shrimp eggs in port being loaded onto a truck.

Brine shrimp tug heading out of port.

Some areas, as in the Canyonlands of southern Utah, potholes exist that after filling from rain, quickly come to life with a type of "shrimp" that appears very similar to the brine shrimp. Being well adapted to long periods of drought, they become dormant when the water dries up, but readily reappear after water is provided. [Note: Don't confuse these creatures with mosquito larva.]

Brine Flies

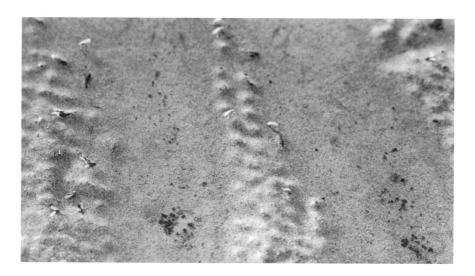

Brine flies are insects, slightly smaller than a housefly, that hatch from tiny eggs within the warm, shallow waters of Great Salt Lake. In this larva stage they feed on algae and bacteria. Then they enter a floating pupa stage from which they hatch and swarm over the lake and its shores by the billions. If conditions are right, this process takes place in 36 hours. The very hot, consistent temperatures of mid to late summer seem to be ideal. Otherwise, with temperature, salinity or other variations, the process can be delayed.

Brine flies can be a nuisance due to numbers alone, but are not attracted to humans, don't bite, are not attracted to human food, and do not transmit disease. When disturbed, they fly close to the ground, and are usually associated with wet areas even slightly inland from the lake. Once hatched into their final adult stage as flies, they live another 3-4 days. Brine fly pupa carrying their air supply in a bubble, feed on algae below the water's surface. Their pupae cases are attached to "reefs" on the lake's bottom. When ready to emerge, the creamy white adult flies make a hole in the pupa case and pop out at the water's surface. They turn a dark gray color as their new skin hardens. Pupae are dislodged from the lake's floor by storms and blown to the shores by wind. Indians who gathered the pupae for food called them "Koo-Ts'abe." Gulls are often seen with their mouths wide open, half running and half flying along the shores of Great Salt Lake collecting and consuming brine flies.

Easily accessible on the lake's surface, shorelines and surrounding areas, brine flies not only provide food for many birds visiting Great Salt Lake, but are also a food source for spiders, reptiles and other small creatures adjacent to the lake. Their pupas greatly supplemented the Indian's diet, providing protein often lacking. Early explorers could tell when the harvest was on by the change in the Indian's appearance and general health, evident in skin tone, shiny hair, and expression.

Brine Fly Larva

Many consider insects pests and something to be eliminated from the environment, but a lot of species and complete ecosystems depend on them for survival. Brine flies greatly contribute to the health of the environment by removing waste in consuming and converting over 120,000 tons of organic material to useable food for wildlifc. Brine shrimp also significantly contribute to this environmental recycling process. Other insects, such as mosquitoes, Midge Flies, gnats ("no-see-ums") and May Flies are common around the shores of Great Salt Lake. Supported by the fresh water marshy areas, they provide a food supply for other birds as swallows and fly-catchers, or even flying mammals such as bats. All parts of nature play an important role in the ecosystem and its cycle of life, contributing to the corresponding food chain. Algae is consumed by brine flies and brine shrimp, and then they are consumed by birds. The birds, their eggs and young are devoured by fox, snakes, weasels, skunks, raccoons, and other mammals.

An important consideration:

Due to salinity changes caused by the railroad causeway's division of Great Salt Lake, half of the lake is rendered incapable of producing a food supply—one supporting a well-balanced ecosystem and huge migratory bird population. One may wonder if accurate and complete records were kept prior to the causeway's construction to determine the impact on wildlife/bird populations existing prior.

Migratory Bird Populations

Over 257 species of birds rely on Great Salt Lake for survival. Many stop on both their northern and southern migratory voyages. Some, as the California Gull, stay all summer. The Eared Grebe actually doubles its size in weight to replace its feathers and gain energy reserves in preparation for its migratory flight to southern Baja California, Mexico. The Wilson's Phalarope travels 5,000 miles, and the Red-necked Phalarope travels 6,000 miles in their migratory flights from the arctic to South America.

California Gull

California Gulls have been held in high regard since they destroyed a plague of crickets that threatened the crops of Mormon pioneers in 1848. Thus, as a result, they were deemed the Utah state bird. Birds as the California Gull are scavengers, and don't have to leave the lake to feed. However, pelicans, herons, cormorants and terns are fish-eaters that rely on fresh water areas for food. Pelicans, for example, work especially hard to secure enough food for themselves and their young. Prevalent on Gunnison Island, they must often travel 80-100 miles to reach and return from fresh water areas for fish. While they are gone, other members of the rookery tend their young. Upon a parent's return, the young pelican places its entire upper body through its parent's mouth, dipping into and eating the stored food (stomach contents) the parent has secured.

Pelicans work as a team to herd fish.

Among some of the birds most commonly seen are the American Avocet, Long-billed Curlew, Black-necked Stilt, Killdeer, White-faced Ibis, plovers, Great Blue Heron, California Gull (and several other species of gulls to a lesser extent), Snowy Egret, willets, terns, and Western Grebe. And along the lake's borders in the brackish reed areas, both Red-winged and Yellow-headed Blackbirds are common.

Black-necked Stilt

Many species have adapted by a long evolutionary process to a specialized diet and ecological niche. As with some birds, this specialized adaptation applies to certain crustaceans and insects. Such is the case with many shorebirds that have developed specialized physical and behavioral characteristics. The avocet, for example, with a long, narrow, slightly curved bill, sweeps slightly under the water's surface back and forth to collect brine shrimp and aquatic insects. The Black-necked Stilt, with its long straight bill, uses a fast, short pecking motion to capture its food.

Through a bio-genetic process, lasting many centuries, a species becomes better equipped and more efficient at procuring a particular species as a main food source. However, if this food source is threatened, the special adaptation (and corresponding dependency) becomes a disadvantage. The species is left with no way to cope. The special and specific adaptation of the species, which took thousands of years to perfect, is no longer useful and other food sources are not accepted. If brine flies and brine shrimp were no longer available, many Great Salt Lake shorebirds could no longer exist.

The corixid is a type of small water beetle that prefers a less saline aquatic environment than is usually offered by the lake. It is part of the family Corixidae that is commonly called water boatman, found in the brackish pools along seashores above the high tidemark. Similarly, the corixid, prevalent in brackish areas adjacent to the lake, enters Great Salt Lake. Most species feed on algae and small aquatic organisms. Certain varieties prey on the brine shrimp.

Algae

Twenty-nine species of algae are known to exist within Great Salt Lake. Several are consumed by the brine flies and brine shrimp.

Algae and brine shrimp eggs deposited on shoreline.

Brine shrimp eggs behind caked algae frosted by brine flies.

Bacteria

Bacteria living on the lake's floor produce calcium carbonate, and build structures resembling, to a small extent, coral reefs of the ocean. Tufa is calcium carbonate that also accumulates by fresh water influence, evident from previous lake levels.

The conical formations within Mono Lake, California—a cousin to Great Salt Lake—are formed from this process as calcium-rich spring water rises through the lake that is rich in bicarbonate. The calcium and bicarbonate combine, precipitating out as limestone. With the formation cylinders encircling the fresh water eventually to the lake's surface, these cones can rise to the highest water level the lake has reached if the level is sustained for a long enough period. When the lake recedes, these towers are left above the water's surface.

Mono Lake, California.

Lake Smell

An associated "lake smell" surrounds the lake. The odor, only originating from the shores, not the lake water, is derived from decomposing organic material, consisting mainly of algae and brine fly pupae cases. Dead birds are in the mix, especially after avian cholera and botulism outbreaks take place, as was the case in '93 and '94.

Fish carcasses are also common, mostly from carp getting trapped within the saline confines of the lake. They are carried in areas of fresh, or brackish, water that become surrounded by salt water, leaving the fish within to succumb to the saltwater environment. This material, once disturbed by wind, water, or other means, will emit a strong, unpleasant odor, not uncommon to the urban areas surrounding Great Salt Lake.

The *Pea Soup* Effect

From spring until early fall Great Salt Lake goes through a series of cycles. Beginning with the warm weather, bacteria and algae build up until the water becomes a greenish color. This condition lasts until the brine flies and brine shrimp hatch and multiply enough to devour this massive food supply. Then, once the food supply is depleted, their numbers decrease, and the cycle starts over again. These cycles will continue to occur throughout the summer until fall. However, the first is usually the most impressive, since the algae and bacteria levels build up more extensively in the spring before the brine shrimp and brine flies have a chance to hatch and consume them.

Transition Zone of the Great Salt Lake

A very gradual decline in elevation exists from land towards a large, but very shallow salty body of water (34' at the deepest point, with an average lake elevation of 4,200'). Due to this, the Great Salt Lake harbors an immense amount of wetlands that provide nesting, food and shelter for birds and small mammals, and contributes a habitat that transforms to a saltwater environment. However, this aquatic influence only exists where the major tributaries enter the lake. In other areas of the same proximity to the lake, the environment is quite different. A salt desert exists.

Halophytes

Halophytes are plants that tolerate a high salinity level. They exist adjacent to, and within, the Great Salt Lake.

Aquatic, and Pinkish Coloration of Northern Arm
Algae and bacteria within the Great Salt Lake, with Blue-green algae to a lesser extent, are halophytic. The northern arm of the lake, at an average salinity between 25 and 27.3%, harbors mostly the reddish-pigmented algae and bacteria, which gives it the distinct pinkish coloration.

Shores
Salt bush, pickle weed, grease wood, ink weed, iodine bush, sedge and salt grass are halophytes. Fragmyties and tamarisk are also salt tolerant. However, to survive, many of these plant species need some fresh water influence adjacent to the lake.

Pickle weed growing amongst brine fly pupae cases and salt crystals.

Marshes, Sloughs and Wetlands

While Great Salt Lake provides brine shrimp and brine flies as food sources, adjacent wetlands provide excellent nesting habitat for hundreds of thousands of birds. Fresh water entering the lake is complemented by a very gradual decline in elevation to form large wetland areas.

Mother Killdeer defending her nest.

Killdeer eggs within nest.

Killdeer chicks

Dragon Fly--a common inhabitant of marshy areas surrounding Great Salt

"Marshes are the single richest ecosystem yet defined in terms of available energy, even when compared with most types of intensive farming" (Odum 1963).

Since these areas produce an abundance of food, the Fremont built their villages and camps within the wetlands adjacent to the lake.

"Site density in these marshes is as high or higher than any other region in Utah (including those occupied by the Anasazi) and it is almost impossible to distinguish one site from another along the length of the levees because they are so numerous" (Madsen, D.).

Development of agricultural lands for housing and road construction is one of the most vital environmental concerns threatening the wetlands and adjacent farmlands surrounding Great Salt Lake.

Natural Phenomenon Related to Change in Lake's Ecology

When Great Salt Lake's water level rose between 1983 to 1987, the salinity level became so diluted by fresh water (at about 5.5%) that the Rainwater Killi fish--a small species of fish that lives in brackish water--entered the lake in 1986 from Timpie Springs. It was able to live in Great Salt Lake for a brief time period--about a year or so--until the lake receded and regained a salinity beyond its level of tolerance. Locals recall looking into the lake and being startled by seeing fish in a familiar aquatic environment never before containing anything larger than a brine shrimp.

Temperatures below Freezing in a Liquid Form

The surface water temperature of Great Salt Lake varies from the upper 20s F. in January to about 80 degrees F. in early August. Although the temperatures are often below freezing during the winter months, the water does not freeze due to the water's high salinity level. When the water temperature dips to the 20s, however, this causes very dangerous boating conditions. Hypothermia immediately takes effect upon entry. A person accidentally falling into this extremely cold water can only survive a few minutes, and must be quickly rescued to recover.

Ice Collection on the Lake

Ice from the lake's surface heaped upon the shore by wind and wave action.

How can ice exist on the Great Salt Lake if salt water, especially of this high salinity level, doesn't freeze? Because fresh water, which is lighter than salt water, freezes before mixing with the salt water. This occurs by either tributaries directly depositing ice or fresh water into the lake, or by springs within the lake expelling water that freezes upon reaching the lake's surface when winter lake conditions are very still.

Icebergs have reached 30' high on the lake, as witnessed and demonstrated by Charles Stoddard in the following photo.

(Used by permission of the Utah Historical Society.)

Chapter Eleven

An Inland Sea

Great Salt Lake is the most extensive salt water body in the Western hemisphere. Similar, to the Great Lakes, but smaller, yet more isolated in a desert region, it significantly influences major weather storms and creates its own regional weather patterns.

Comparisons with Other Salt Water Bodies

	Salinity Level (Parts per Thousand)	Coverage (Square Miles)
Caspian Sea (Russia, Iran)	11	170,000
Aral Sea (Russia)	10	25,000
Lake Balkhash (Russia)	2.8	7,115
Great Salt Lake	140 Gilbert Bay	1,700
Salton Sea (California	44	380
Dead Sea (Israel)	220	390
Mono Lake (California)	78	71

Besides high salinity, ice bergs, brine shrimp and real sea gulls (mostly California gulls making their annual visit), Great Salt Lake defends itself as an inland sea in other ways. Although land-locked, it has the ability to cleanse itself, even with the added burden of human discharge. To the surprise of many, recent studies have shown Great Salt Lake to be very clean. This has been mainly attributed to the brine flies, algae, brine shrimp, mineral salts, and other qualities that contribute to the breaking-down process, which is also evident in the ocean. As a true inland sea, the Great Salt Lake masters an age-old environment, with many tell-tale ancient migrations relying on this aquatic monarch for their existence.

Although fluctuating, a consistency of patterns reveal a

relative stability in nature that is rooted in biology. Nature seems to know there is an acceptable salinity level matching a required consistency. Brine shrimp refuse to hatch, and become dormant for many years, unless conditions are favorable. Salinity level and temperature are both important factors, but salinity level is the most influential factor since the time of year usually determines water temperature. However, a cool spring could mean a late hatch and less food sources for early spring migrations. An early winter could have the same effect on fall migrations.

Buoyancy

Due to a very high salinity, Great Salt Lake offers the effects of increased buoyancy. Famed for the effects of *bobbing*

Revealing the buoyancy factor, two boiled eggs are placed into jars, the right at about 25% salinity and the left in fresh water.

like a cork, Great Salt Lake is notorious for attracting many bathing visitors who want to experience the effect. The popularity, however, has decreased with the absence of lake resorts and bathing access to the lake. Saltair and Antelope Island both offer limited access and facilities.

Salinity Level

The average salt content of Great Salt Lake is about 25%, which figure is derived from combining the whole lake's salinity. This is about 8 times saltier than the ocean, which is at 3%. With the lake's salinity level changing during wet and dry cycles, the lowest salinity level ever recorded is 5% and the highest is 27%. The mineral saturation point is 27.3%, being the highest concentration possible when mineral salts crystallize. The Dead Sea is at this level.

Lake Minerals

Sodium chloride, common table salt, makes up the largest percentage of mineral salt within Great Salt Lake, and represents the highest amount of mineral salt extracted from the lake, at 400,000 tons per year.

Akzo salt plant bordering I-80.

Magnesium, due to its light weight, but strong qualities, is a metal used in airplane construction and for automobile wheels ("mags."). It is a mineral extracted from Great Salt Lake in the form of salt, and is essential in our diet. Once refined, the metal is shipped by railroad cars. Chlorine is extracted in the same process, and shipped by railroad tankers. Calcium and potassium are also minerals extracted from the evaporation ponds.

Calcium, often seen in the form of tufa and the major component of oolitic sand (calcium carbonate), is another large mineral constituent of the lake. Other consumptive sources of this mineral exist in food sources such as milk.

Both chlorine and potash (potassium) contribute to water softeners and laundry detergent. Other combined uses for magnesium, calcium, phosphorous and potassium include salt/mineral blocks for cattle and other livestock, nutrients/mineral supplements for human consumption, and fertilizer.

Chlorine is used to purify water for human consumption, as laundry bleach, and a cleanser.

A Changing Shoreline/Depth

Correlating to salinity level and area coverage, the size of Great Salt Lake has varied from about 700 to 2,400 square miles. The lake averages about 90 miles in length from north to south and about 40 miles in width from east to west. But it is very shallow in comparison to its surface size. Existing on the floor of what used to be Lake Bonneville, Great Salt Lake expands over an immense plate-like area. A rise or fall in lake elevation by only a couple of feet horizontally extends or recedes the lake's shoreline by miles. With an average elevation of 4,200 feet, the lake has a maximum depth of 34 feet, and averages a depth of 13 feet.

Cycles and Seasonal Variations

The lake's depth changes during multi-wet or multi-dry cycles, as was the case between 1983 to 1987, and significantly fluctuates on an annual basis.

Beginning in 1982, and lasting through 1987, the region experienced a cool, wet cycle, with the lake peaking slightly under 4,212'. This effect in the plate-like topography covered many additional miles in a horizontal direction on all shorelines of the lake. The horizontal increase in the lake's size consumed and devastated marshlands and thousands of acres of wildlife habitat.

A seasonal variation in depth can result in a 3-4 foot fluctuation during a normal year. The lake rises in the spring due to precipitation and early snow-melt, and continues rising into early summer due to higher temperatures and additional snow-melt. Beginning in mid-summer, the water level begins to fall due to snow-pack depletion and high evaporation rates, and continues to recede into the fall, but then stabilizes in the winter. A constant juggling act between precipitation and evaporation rates is preformed by the lake.

Great Salt Lake Water Sources

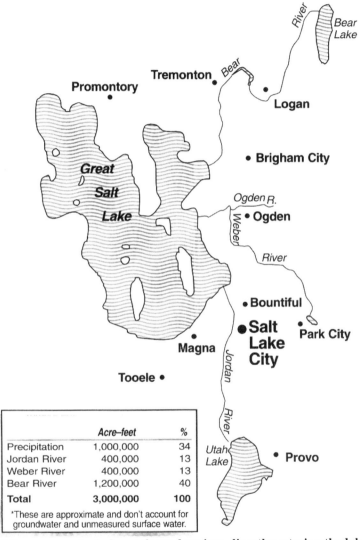

	Acre–feet	%
Precipitation	1,000,000	34
Jordan River	400,000	13
Weber River	400,000	13
Bear River	1,200,000	40
Total	**3,000,000**	**100**

*These are approximate and don't account for groundwater and unmeasured surface water.

Other sources include creeks and springs directly entering the lake.

Weather

The weather associated with Great Salt Lake is unique to the region. Tornadoes occasionally form over the lake and head inland, as did one in 1999 that damaged property, injured many people and killed one person in Salt Lake City.

What's referred to as a Tooele Twister will often originate in the Tooele area when a larger storm enters the Great Salt Lake vicinity. Due to the local geography and the way a storm approaches, its intensity is often magnified. Waves on Great Salt Lake are known to reach 18' high during severe storms.

Isolated storm moving east across Great Salt Lake.

Micro-bursts are isolated storms often caused by single clouds, and are common upon the Great Salt Lake. Striking very quickly, they bring cloudbursts, extreme winds and very rough water in short duration, about 15 to 20 minutes, causing dangerous conditions for boaters.

The Lake Effect

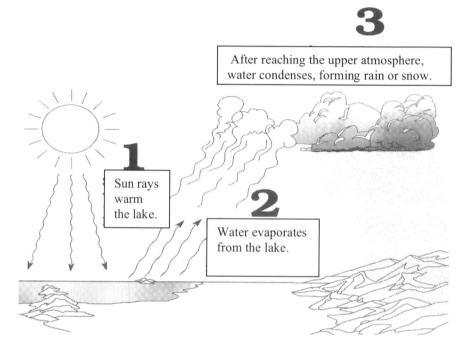

3

After reaching the upper atmosphere, water condenses, forming rain or snow.

1

Sun rays warm the lake.

2

Water evaporates from the lake.

The lake creates its own weather patterns at a local level. Although cooler during the day, the lake is warmer at night during the summer, with these contrasts in temperature often causing a wind. The cooler temperatures of the Rocky Mountains (Wasatch Range) in contrast to the warmer lake temperatures often create winds and other micro-climatic weather changes. The "lake effect" also occurs when the lake's water temperature is comparatively warmer than the winter air, when evaporation significantly contributes to heavy snowfalls. This same phenomenon occurs in the Great Lakes Region.

Chapter Twelve

Strange Phenomena

As six-sided construction is evident in the bee's honey comb, a six-sided effect also lies within the structure of the salt polygons evident on the surface of the salt flats in areas lying beyond the thick, solid salt surface used by the Bonneville Raceway. As a result of evaporation and the process of upward capillarity, mineral salts are deposited on the earth's surface. The drier the surface gets, the more distinct and stronger are the salt accumulations and crystallization, which process builds up pressure until it's released by the surface breaking into six-sided symmetrical formations, all uniquely corresponding to thousands of other hexagons.

The Power of Salt

As water during the winter months can freeze and crack pipes, the same power of freezing expansion occurs when water gets trapped in rocks and breaks them apart. (The water crystallization effect is seen in snowflakes, which one would seldom view as such a powerful source.) The power of crystal expansion also exists in salt, evidenced not only in the polygons, but by fence posts acting as sponge-like siphons, as the water laden in mineral salts is absorbed into the wood. When the wood dries, the salt crystallizes (expands), splintering the wood.

Splintered wood. Acting as a wick for salt water, the fence post demonstrates the expansion power of salt crystallization.

Expansion cracks thin layers of salt on the ground's surface.

These "octopus-like" formations within the Great Salt Lake Desert are caused from the drying process of a mixture of clay and mud with salt.

Moving Rocks

This phenomenon occurs in other salt flats, such as those in Death Valley, and is believed to be caused by wind after a rain storm. The wet salt offers little resistance to high winds that push the rocks over a hard, smooth and slippery surface.

Another Similar Lake Environment

A cousin to Great Salt Lake, Mono Lake, located in eastern California, is a remnant of ancient Lake Lahontan. It too has brine shrimp, which are harvested, and brine, or what are referred to there as alkali, flies.

Tufa Mounds

Due to upward capillarity, salt is deposited on top of these tufa mounds. (Used by permission of the Utah Historical Society.)

Devil's Slide

Devil's Slide--a geological formation located on I-84 southeast of Ogden.

Salt precipitates out above the water line, as evaporation leaves a "toadstool-like" formation.

Conclusion

After a few samples, one begins to experience the many dimensions of the Great Salt Lake area. More discoveries lie in wait as one may choose to further investigate the wonders of this region.

Bibliography

Ambrose, Steven E., *Nothing like it in the world: The Men Who Built The Transcontinental Railroad 1863-1869*. New York: Simon & Schuster, 2000.

Brinkley, Alan, *The Unfinished Nation—A Concise History of the American People*. New York: Columbia University, McGraw-Hill, Inc., 1993.

Crampton, Gregory C. and Madsen, Steven K., *In Search of the Spanish Trail, Santa Fe to Los Angeles, 1829-1848*. Salt Lake City: Gibbs Smith, 1994.

DeLafosse, Peter H., Editor, *Trailing the Pioneers*. Logan: Utah State University Press, and Utah Crossroads, Oregon-California Trails Association, 1994.

DeVoto, Bernard, *the Year of Decision 1846*. Boston: Houghton Mifflin Company, 1942.

Egan, Ferol, *Fremont, Explorer for a Restless Nation*. Reno: University of Nevada Press, 1977.

Gwyn, Ph.D., Wallace J., *Great Salt Lake—a Scientific, Historical and Economic Overview*. Salt Lake City: Department of Natural Resources, Utah Geological and Mineral Survey Bulletin 116, 1980.

Hassibe, W.R. and Keck, W.G., *The Great Salt Lake*. Denver: U.S. Geological Survey, Revised Printing. 1991.

Holt, Clayton, *History of Antelope Island (1840-1995)*. Syracuse: The Syracuse Historical Commission. Third edition, 1996.

Madsen, D., B., *The Shoshoni Frontier and the Bear River Massacre*. Salt Lake City: University of Utah, 1985.

May, Dean L., Utah: *A People's History*. Salt Lake City: University of Utah Press, 1978.

Maxwell, James A., Editor. *America's Fascinating Indian Heritage— The First Americans: Customs, Art, History and How They Lived.* Pleasantville: Reader's Digest Association, 1978.

Miller, David E., *Great Salt Lake—Past and Present.* Sixth edition. Salt Lake City: Publishers Press, 1997.

Nevins, Allen, *Fremont, Pathmaker of the West.* Lincoln: University of Nebraska, 1995.

Stewart, George R., *Ordeal By Hunger.* Boston: Pocket Books, 1936.

Stokes, William Lee, *The Great Salt Lake.* Salt Lake City: Starstone Publishing Co., 1984.

Stum, Marlin, *Visions of Antelope Island and Great Salt Lake.* Logan: Utah State University Press, 1999.

The Great Salt Lake, America's Inland Sea (video). Ogden: Concepts Wisdom Enterprises, 1988.

Vestal, Stanley, *Jim Bridger Mountain Man.* Lincoln: University of Nebraska Press, 1946.

Warner, Ted J., Editor, Chavez, Fray Angelico, Translator, *The Dominguez-Escalante Journal.* Salt Lake City: University of Utah Press, 1995.

Wharton, Tom, "Utah's Amazing Inland Sea." Salt Lake City: *Salt Lake Tribune,* Special Edition, 1992.

Williams, Terry Tempest, The Desert Sea Seminar. Salt Lake City: University of Utah, Fall, 1993.

Yenne, Bill, Editor, *The Opening of the American West.* Secaucus: Chartwell Books, Inc., 1993.

Wormser, Richard, *The Iron Horse—How the Railroads Changed America.* New York: Walker and Company, 1993.

Author with his daughter, Melinda, at Chaco Canyon.

Alan Millard has a background of knowledge and experience gained from several natural resource agencies. His first appointment was with the National Park Service as a back-country ranger in Colorado. After this, he worked as a Washington State Park Ranger along the Columbia River near Astoria, Oregon. Then he worked for the Bureau of Land Management in Nevada as a supervisor over a district's campgrounds and wilderness study areas. He later became a Utah State Park Ranger, with his last appointment at Antelope Island State Park as a ranger/naturalist and visitor center manager. He has also gained knowledge and experience from his personal research, visitation and exploration of the most renown, and many remote, cultural sites—both occupied and abandoned. He is currently teaching at Weber State University.

Mr. Millard has a Bachelor's degree in Natural Resources from Western Washington University, a Master's degree in Organizational Management from the University of Phoenix, and graduate work completed in Anthropology from the University of Utah, with additional graduate coursework completed in education, English and history from Weber State University. He has been actively involved in various projects designed to preserve local history and the area's environment. He served as an inter-agency committee member in an effort to preserve the historical, cultural and natural resource values of the Wendover area, including such interests as Danger Cave and Juke Box Cave, the Enola Gay Hanger, the Bonneville Salt Flats, Donner-Reed/Hastings Cut-off Trail, Pilot Peak landmark, and the Bonneville Speedway.

Mr. Millard developed a self-perpetuating miniature environment of the Great Salt Lake, complete with brine shrimp, brine flies and algae, and secured the Fremont Island archaeological exhibit (Stoddard Collection), for which project he helped prepare and write the text. These exhibits are on display at the Antelope Island Visitor Center, and are often visited by university students and professors, as well as the general public.

The professor has had many articles published, been a guest speaker on several radio talk shows, conducted news announcements on local events, and appeared on television for environmental news shorts. He has also conducted many presentations and educational seminars, and has been a guest speaker at writers', and other, conferences. He has edited natural resource publications, and is one of the co-authors of *Great Salt Lake–an overview of change*, Gywnn. Mr. Millard has been involved in parental/fathers'/men's organizations, and has conducted many presentations and speaking engagements pertaining to both political issues and natural resource education. He is also the author of *Equality: A Man's Claim*, which is a comprehensive, 563-page book addressing modern-day prejudices against men and the equality issue from the male perspective.